The Most Difficult Choice

MW00424391

Would you...
be machine-gunned to death with Lite-Brite pegs

OR

be wrapped up and suffocated in a giant Fruit Roll-Up?

Would you rather have sex with...
R2D2

OR

C3PO?

Would you rather...
have a Velcro beard

OR

or an afro of Crazy Straws?

Would you rather...?

Pop Culture Edition

Over **300** Preposterous Pop Culture Dilemmas to Ponder

Justin Heimberg & David Gomberg

Published by Falls Media
565 Park Avenue, Suite 11E
New York, NY 10021

First Printing, June 2007
10 9 8 7 6 5 4 3 2
© Copyright Justin Heimberg and David Gomberg, 2007
All Rights Reserved

Would you rather...?® is a registered trademark owned by Falls Media

Printed in Canada
Design by Tom Schirtz

ISBN-10 0-9740439-7-4
ISBN-13 978-0-9740439-7-5

To All The Girls We've Loved Before
(but who didn't like us "in that way")

Acknowledgments

We did this one pretty much ourselves, when it comes down to it.

Contents

Who Says We've Lost It?

When we wrote the original *Would You Rather...?* book more than ten years ago, we were but young and naïve college students, and the weight of the world had not yet crushed our spirits. *Would You Rather...?* was full of inside jokes, obscure pop culture references, and the type of inspired visceral "random" humor that young people love and older jaundiced generations despise. We took as much joy from those who didn't get it as from those who did.

Now, we ourselves are a bit older. Some might contend then—quite logically—that we are not immune; that we will have inevitably lost that wild, unrestrained, silly instinctual sense of humor concomitant with youth. Nonsense. Take for example, this pearl of absurdity we recently came up with:

Would you rather...
obtain a home loan with a 5/1 adjustable interest rate and a 9.75% cap
OR
a 30-year fixed-rate loan at 6.25% with a 15% down payment?
Things to consider: likely escalation in interest rates, the inevitable aftermath of Greenspan's reign as Federal Reserves Chairman

Zinger! That's an excerpt from *Would You Rather... Home Loan Mortgage Edition,* just one of many hilarious whacked-out over-the-top absurd volumes on the way, such as *Would You Rather...?: Personal Taxes Computation Edition, Would You Rather...?: Selling Out to the Lowest Common Denominator Edition,* and *Would You Rather...?: Love & Sex Giving Way To Subdued Comfort of Companionship Edition.*

Critics also claim that as you grow older, you grow out of touch with the current popular culture. Really? Is that why we just watched the rap and used the internet.com?

Suffice to say, we are still quite "with it." We have our finger on America's fat-wristed pulse, so please enjoy these questions concerning what is on everyone's mind these days: fights to the death with toys, mascot sex, and former NBA seven-footers in drag.

Enjoy.

How To Use This Book

Sit around with a bunch of friends and read a question to each other, discussing it until the momentum of the conversation fades into awkward silence and nervous glances. Everybody must choose. As the Deity proclaims, YOU MUST CHOOSE! That's the whole premise of this thing. It forces you to really think about the options. Once everyone has chosen, move on to the next question. It's that simple. We have provided a few things to consider when deliberating each question, but don't restrict yourself to these topics, as much of the fun comes from imagining the different ways your choice will affect your life. If you receive a question directed at females, and you are a male (or vice versa), you can do one of several things: a) move on to another question, b) answer the question anyway, or c) panic.

CHAPTER 1

SEX

These are the circumstances. A powerful deity descends from on high and presents you with a diabolical dilemma concerning your sex life: a horrific affliction, a bizarre lust-laden experience, or, if you're lucky, an enticing opportunity. Always a believer in human free will, the Deity allows you the choice between two possible fates.

"I'm bringing sexy back; Them other boys don't know how to act"

– John Quincy Adams

Would you rather have sex with...

Leonardo Dicaprio *OR* Russell Crowe?

the old James Bond (Sean Connery in his prime) *OR* the new James Bond (Daniel Craig)?

a soft and tender Tony Danza *OR* a fast and furious Mr. Belvedere?

George Clooney *OR* John Goodman if they exchanged weights?

Dick Cheney *OR* the Burger King mascot?

Would you rather have sex with...

Charlize Theron *OR* Lucy Liu?

Mandy Moore *OR* Jaime Pressly?

an unenthusiastic Ashlee Simpson *OR* a nasty Nancy Pelosi?

Natalie Portman *OR* Jennifer Lopez if they had each other's butts?

YOU MUST CHOOSE!

Would you rather...

have LEGO-man-head genital warts

OR

glow-in-the-dark herpes outbreaks?

Things to consider: studded for her pleasure, auto-night-light

Would you rather...

have a scrotum that puffs up like a car airbag whenever you get scared (breasts for women)

OR

a beat-boxing anus?

SEX

YOU MUST CHOOSE!

3

Would you rather...

speak in the voice and style of Jar Jar Binks during sex

OR

have blurred, pixilated privates like they use to censor nudity on TV?

Things to consider: "Me love you long time!"; benefits of blurring if you are a poorly-endowed man

Would you rather...

have sex with Velma from Scooby Doo

OR

Ms. Pac-Man?

Things to consider: orgasmic exclamations of "Jinkies!," insatiable appetite, Clyde

YOU MUST CHOOSE!

Would you rather...

have to solve a moderate-level Sudoku before unwrapping and using a condom

OR

only be able to maintain an erection (men)/reach orgasm (women) by singing the *Family Ties* theme song over and over?

YOU MUST CHOOSE!

Would you rather...

have sex with Hugh Jackman and get the mumps

OR

have sex with John Madden and get a $200 gift certificate to JCPenney?

Would you rather...

have sex with Carmen Electra and lose a finger

OR

have sex with Janet Reno and gain permanent immunity from speeding tickets?

YOU MUST CHOOSE!

Would you rather only be able to have sex while playing...

"Eye of the Tiger" *OR* "Hava Nagila?"

Buffalo Springfield's "Stop, Hey, What's That Sound" *OR* Beethoven's "Ninth Symphony?"

"The Wheels on the Bus Go Round and Round" *OR* William Hung's rendition of "She Bangs?"

the *Star Trek* theme *OR* the *Schindler's List* theme?

an audio book of *Angela's Ashes OR* recordings of a senile man trying to find his way out of a K-Mart?

SEX

YOU MUST CHOOSE!

Would you rather...

have your computer desktop wallpaper be a picture of a naked Warren Sapp **OR**

have to always use the IM screen name "BallsMcGee" (including in professional situations)?

Upon orgasm, would you rather...

ejaculate au jus **OR** a small coiled novelty snake akin to those found in April Fool's Day prank peanut brittle jars?

a mist of Lysol **OR** Easy Cheese?

Skittles **OR** Broom Hilda dialogue bubbles?

YOU MUST CHOOSE!

Would you rather have phone sex with...

Bill O'Reilly *OR* Busta Rhymes?

William Faulkner *OR* Kermit the Frog?

Nelson Mandela and Posh Spice (on conference) *OR* Anna Kournikova and Squiggy from *Laverne & Shirley*?

Would you rather have phone sex with...

Celine Dion *OR* Maya Angelou?

a severely congested Alyssa Milano *OR* Soledad O'Brien?

Penelope Cruz and Larry Bird (on conference) *OR* Arianna Huffington and World Wrestling Entertainment's Jim Ross?

Things to consider: misunderstandings due to accents, arm-drag take-downs

SEX

YOU MUST CHOOSE!

9

Would you rather...

have to masturbate wearing a condom

OR

have to masturbate to pre-1979 sex symbols?

Would you rather...

have "buffering" to your masturbation fantasies like a slow streaming video on the web

OR

have any dialogue in your masturbation fantasies spoken in Korean?

Things to consider: Other books that had full pages devoted to masturbation: *Crime and Punishment, Goodnight Moon, There's a Wocket in My Pocket, The Biography of Harriet Tubman*

YOU MUST CHOOSE!

Would you rather...

have a penis that doubles as a microphone

OR

have a working cable TV video screen on your taint?

Things to consider: using mirrors to watch TV, occasional microphone feedback

"'Taint your balls... 'taint your ass." – William Shakespeare

SEX

YOU MUST CHOOSE!

Would you rather attend an orgy with...

Congress *OR* a horde of Jawas?

Smurfs *OR* Snorks?

your high school graduating class *OR* your high school teachers at the age they were at the time of your graduation?

Would you rather...

eliminate PDA's (as in "public displays of affection")

OR

eliminate PDA's (as in people using "personal digital assistants" when in public)?

YOU MUST CHOOSE!

Would you rather...

(women read as **have a partner who has...**)
have a penis that can change circumference size

OR

that can change length?

Would you rather...

have sex with all celebrities with last names that begin with "L" *OR* "B"?

"G" *OR* "R"?

"Zax..." *OR* "Cyru..."?

YOU MUST CHOOSE!

Would you rather...

have sex with someone with the body of Pamela Anderson, the face of
Queen Elizabeth, and the feet of Yao Ming

OR

the face of Angelina Jolie, the body of Rosie O'Donnell, and the hair of
Jimmy Johnson?

Would you rather...

have a three-way with Patrick Dempsey now and '80's Patrick Dempsey circa
Can't By Me Love

OR

River Phoenix when he was 18, and River Phoenix if he were alive today?

YOU MUST CHOOSE!

Would you rather have sex with...

Kate Moss *OR* Fergie?

Helen Mirren *OR* Queen Latifah?

Judi Dench *OR* Tyra Banks if she was on fire?

Chloe Sevigny if she were deep-fried *OR* Paula Abdul if she had severe irritable bowl syndrome?

Dakota Fanning in ten years *OR* the starting 5 of the Tennessee Volunteers woman's basketball team?

Would you rather have sex with...

McDreamy *OR* McSteamy?

Macpherson *OR* McGowan?

McDonald *OR* McCheese?

McAsymmetrical *OR* McAdhesive?

YOU MUST CHOOSE!

15

Would you rather...

have a TiVo that displays information and exact timing regarding the occurrence and quality of nudity and sex for all shows

OR

have a Microsoft Help Icon that talks dirty to you?

Things to consider: paper clip fetishes, market as "the TiVo Masturbation Guide" (patent pending)

YOU MUST CHOOSE!

Pop Culture Pubes

Would you rather...

have pubic hair that wriggled like worms

OR

have a pube-blot (a different inkblot-like pattern each day)?

Would you rather...

have a Flock of Seagulls style for your pubic hair

OR

a Raleigh Fingers mustache style?

Things to consider: Other works that have dedicated an entire page to pubic hair:
Hamlet, *Rapunzel 2: The Revenge*, the Articles of Confederation,
Where's Waldo?, *Band of Brothers*

YOU MUST CHOOSE!

Would you rather...

have a three-way with TomKat (Tom Cruise, Katie Holmes) *OR* Brangelina (Brad Pitt and Angelina Jolie)?

the old Beniffer (Ben Affleck and J-Lo) *OR* the new Bennifer (Ben Affleck and Jennifer Garner)?

BobCat (Bob Saget and Catherine Zeta Jones) *OR* Phillary (Dr. Phil and Hillary Duff)?

Dobberts (Lou Dobbs and Julia Roberts) *OR* BoutrosBoutrosHalle (BoutrousBoutrous-Ghali and Halle Berry)?

YOU MUST CHOOSE!

Would you rather...

give oral sex to your wife or girlfriend during menstruation

OR

have conversations about her weight and other sensitive topics during menstruation?

Would you rather...

have a cell phone that is also an mp3 player and a camera

OR

that is also a boomerang and a vibrator?

Things to consider: speaker-phone phone sex, safari trips

YOU MUST CHOOSE!

POP Goes the Culture

The Deity likes the show *Lost*. He wishes his facial hair could grow to such a precisely handsome length revealing rugged good looks instead of having an evil goatee that gives him rugged diabolical looks. In fact, he likes the show so much, he is stranding you on a remote island as well. The good news is that you get someone or something to keep you company.

Would you rather be stuck on a desert island with...

Jack (Matthew Fox) *OR* Sawyer (Josh Holloway)?

daily delivery of the *Washington Post* Comics section *OR* the Obituaries section?

a thesaurus *OR* a copy of a *Plumpers* porn magazine? How about a publication that combines both?

equivocal lumberjacks *OR* taciturn botanists?

a Stomper 4x4 truck toy *OR* an insanity-induced hallucination of guardian angel Mats Wilander?

Would you rather...

BE STUCK ON A DESERT ISLAND WITH SOCRATES

JENNA JAMESON?

CHAPTER

CURSES

The Deity is angry. He's been reading the tabloids and learning about all the celebrity scandals: the out-of-control addictions, the shameless affairs, the life-threatening eating disorders. Aside from the panda, the human race is the most pathetic species on the planet. The Deity desires an outlet for his anger, and that's where you come in. You are to suffer a terrible curse in the form of a horrible deformity, a bizarre behavioral disorder or an irksome inconvenience. The Deity is not without compassion, however, and allows you to choose between two fates.

Would you rather...

have Parmesan cheese dandruff

OR

bubble wrap acne?

Would you rather have your child's high school guidance counselor be...

Tom Sizemore *OR* Simon Cowell?

the *Queer Eye* guys *OR* Apache Chief?

Donald Trump *OR* the hosts from *What Not To Wear*?

Charles Manson *OR* Q-bert?

Things to consider: @#$%!*&!

YOU MUST CHOOSE!

Would you rather...

walk like a runway model all the time

OR

always walk like a runway attendant who is ushering in planes at an airport?

YOU MUST CHOOSE!

Would you rather...

be restricted to using a Big Wheel as your only means of transportation

OR

be forced to cook all your meals in an Easy-Bake oven?

Things to consider: entertaining at home, drive-thru's, office parking lot

Would you rather have a comb-over...

from your eyebrows *OR* from your back hair?

from your ear hair *OR* from your eyelashes?

from your pubic hair *OR* from Dr. Phil's mustache?

YOU MUST CHOOSE!

Would you rather...

appear as Wolf Blitzer in the mirror

OR

have the voice in your head sound like Tommy Chong?

Would you rather...

speak in the rhythm of the *The A-team* theme song

OR

snore the chorus to "Caribbean Queen"?

CURSES

YOU MUST CHOOSE!

27

Would you rather...

have to name your kids after Starbucks beverage sizes

OR

after famous robots?

Things to consider: What if your Grande grows bigger than your Venti?, R2-D2, Seven of Nine, Twiki

Would you rather...

have Monopoly hotel and house pieces for boogers

OR

defecate Rubik's Snakes?

Things to consider: sneezing, position of Rubik's Snake upon egress: the line, the dog, the ball, the swan, etc.

YOU MUST CHOOSE!

Would you rather...

have your echo be in the voice of *Law & Order*'s Sam Waterson

OR

your shadow be on a ten second delay?

Things to consider: Waterson's gravitas, being able to fully enjoy your own shadow puppets

Would you rather...

have Slinkys for arms

OR

Silly Putty for skin?

Thing to consider: reading the newspaper, playing sports

CURSES

YOU MUST CHOOSE!

Would you rather...

everything you eat taste like Bugles

OR

have to take all bowel movements in front of a live studio audience?

Things to consider: eating nutritious foods, laughter, applause, heartfelt "Ahhhhhhs"'s

Would you rather...

have chicken pox that you can peel off and eat like Candy Buttons

OR

have fingerprints that look like a young Willie Aames?

Things to consider: $100 to anyone who can come up with a productive use for the latter

YOU MUST CHOOSE!

Would you rather...

have your head constantly flaming like Ghost Rider's

OR

your scrotum?

YOU MUST CHOOSE!

Would you rather...

be incapable of differentiating between paper shredders and mailboxes *OR* between water fountains and urinals?

between cottage cheese and shampoo *OR* between cell phones and handguns?

between being tired and being lost *OR* between George Gervin and love?

Would you rather...

walk through all doorways as if you were in the heat of an intense limbo competition *OR*
be compelled to make a hula hoop motion whenever you're in the presence of police officers?

YOU MUST CHOOSE!

Would you rather...

sneeze out of your ass

OR

fart out of your nose?

Things to consider: allergy season, crotch rot, skid marks in handkerchiefs

Would you rather...

have a literal handle bar mustache

OR

after the hour of eight PM, become unwaveringly convinced you are Neil Diamond?

YOU MUST CHOOSE!

Would you rather...

be a Boltaur – you have your body's upper half and Manute Bol's lower half

OR

a Nowitskitaur – you have your body's lower half and Dirk Nowitski's upper half?

Would you rather...

have gratuitous product placements in your dreams

OR

have frequent Carrot Top cameos in your dreams?

YOU MUST CHOOSE!

Would you rather...

only be capable of communicating through the use of a Speak & Spell

OR

automatically revert to jazz hands whenever your hands are not in use?

Would you rather...

be compelled to sign off every phone conversation with "Ain't no thang"

OR

invariably tag on a my "My Liege" at the end of all your sentences?

YOU MUST CHOOSE!

WAYS TO MAKE THE OSCARS BETTER

The Deity doesn't much care for the Oscars and its dull, self-congratulatory broadcast. He proposes some changes to the Academy to make things more exciting:

Would you rather...

if an award winner goes over the time limit when giving a thank you speech, they are shot at by snipers in the balcony

OR

require that all presenting pairings are forced to have a baby together?

Would you rather...

have all seat fillers dressed like Boba Fett

OR

have the show hosted by a Chinese guy in some IT department who doesn't speak much English?

CURSES

Mixed Blessings
The Deity on "Random" Play

"You take the good, you take the bad, you take them both and there you have the Facts of Life" – Henry David Thoreau

Would you rather...

be a world renowned Skeeball champion, but melt when exposed to temperatures over 45 degrees Farenheit

OR

never forget a phone number, but only be capable of seeing peripherally?

Would you rather...

never miss a bowling spare but have your upper lip non-responsive to gravity

OR

be an expert whittler but have your nouns come out in German?

YOU MUST CHOOSE!

Would you rather...

be the world's preeminent expert on time-dependent quantum dynamics but always wear a Santa outfit

OR

always be able to escape blame for passing gas but be limited in your TV viewing to re-runs of *Being Bobby Brown*?

YOU MUST CHOOSE!

Would you rather...

have the ability to mute the world but have George Wendt heads for feet

OR

be able to bake succulent brownies but have a variety of Tourettes Syndrome where you randomly exclaim facts about Eli Whitney?

Would you rather...

have pockets filled with an infinite supply of Gummi Bears but be incapable of speaking when not wearing an ascot

OR

have near-perfect knowledge of C++ programming but on Fridays become convinced you are a glass of orange juice and desperately struggle not to spill yourself?

YOU MUST CHOOSE!

Would you rather...

have superior cleavage finding instincts when channel-surfing but have a debilitating fear of right angles?

OR

have thick lustrous hair but believe that you are Dan Aykroyd while it's light out and Pegasus while it's night?

Would you rather...

have the power to solve Rubik's Cubes by putting them down your pants but only have dreams regarding anti-immigration legislation

OR

be immune to the effects of secondhand smoke but give birth to your own left foot?

YOU MUST CHOOSE!

CHAPTER 3

FASHION AND STYLE

Generally, deities are oblivious to the ebb and flow of style. Powerful gods tend to be more concerned with the evolution of their world's humanity than that of hemlines and hairstyles. But this is not your daddy's deity. He's metrosexual. You're no fashion plate Classie Freddie Blassie, and it's time for a make-over, Deity-style.

OULD YOU RATHER...? Pop Culture Edition

Would you rather...

always have to wear ultra-ultra low-riding jeans (waist-line is below the genitals)

OR

ultra high-riding jeans (waist-line is above the nipples)?

Would you rather...

have to keep your keys permanently attached to a loop earring

OR

have to always wear your socks on the outside of your shoes?

YOU MUST CHOOSE!

44

Would you rather...
have literal pig-tails

OR

a literal pony-tail?

YOU MUST CHOOSE!

Would you rather always have to wear...

traditional Samurai garb *OR* a Wonder Twins costume?

Charlie Brown's shirt *OR* a leg bandana á la Chachi from *Happy Days*?

clothes made from pizza cartons *OR* Ziploc bags?

a twenty pound top hat *OR* cross country skis?

cozy feet-encasing pajamas *OR* a blazer featuring Surgeon Generals from history?

Would you rather...

have to sleep in medieval armor pajamas

OR

wear *Braveheart*-style face paint when at work?

YOU MUST CHOOSE!

Would you rather...

have a Velcro beard

OR

an afro of crazy straws?

Things to consider: sleeping on linty sheets, improvising "beer hats"

Would you rather...

have a scar that migrates over your body like an inch worm

OR

be branded on the forehead with the image of Ron Livingston?

YOU MUST CHOOSE!

Would you rather...

wear a giant sunglass monocle in the style of fashionista sunglasses

OR

have a "grill" that is made of Bit-O-Honey and Mastermind game pieces?

Things to consider: Do they have candy grills for kids? (that's a no-brainer)

Would you rather...

have a stitched logo of Constantine Chernenko's face on all your shirts shirt like the alligator on Izod clothes

OR

always have to wear a 6 inch diameter belt buckle of the head of Isaac from the *Love Boat*?

YOU MUST CHOOSE!

Would you rather...

have a nose-piercing with a chain connected to a sparrow

OR

have a massive one hair comb-over that winds back and forth on your head?

Would you rather...

have asymmetrical breast implants

OR

have two equal size breast implants... on your knees?

YOU MUST CHOOSE!

49

You can't misspell "Deity" without the "diet"!

Would you rather...

go on a diet where you use increasingly ineffective eating utensils
(i.e. fork to spork to chopsticks to one chopstick to a slippery ball, etc.)

OR

where you date a passive-aggressive boyfriend who says things like
"We really should work out"?

Would you rather...

only be able to eat orange foods

OR

only be able to eat food starting with the letter "k"?

Things to consider: candy corn bottoms, pumpkin pie, kale, kugel, krelgy-pops

YOU MUST CHOOSE!

Would you rather have a tattoo of...

various geometric formulas *OR* all the U.S. Vice Presidents' heads?

the faces of Bartles and Jaymes on each butt cheek *OR* a gang style tattoo of "N I M O Y" across your chest?

a scratch-and-sniff tattoo of a pickle *OR* a tattoo consisting of the Chinese character for "trite?"

a *Prison Break* map style tattoo of the local mall with a "you are here" marker *OR* an ass crack extension tattoo?

one of those magic-eye 3D things *OR* an ever-changing tattoo that works like Mapquest and shows a map and directions of wherever you have to go at the time?

YOU MUST CHOOSE!

Would you rather...

have a diamond necklace that works as a stethoscope

OR

a tongue-piercing that works as a breath mint?

Would you rather...

have earrings that work as bluetooth headsets

OR

a bracelet that works as a clock?

YOU MUST CHOOSE!

Would you rather always have to wear...

a Klingon uniform and make-up from *Star Trek* OR a Storm Trooper uniform from *Star Wars*?

28 inch stiletto heels OR clothing made from live salamanders?

clothing exclusively patterned in Cheetah print OR adorned with photos of ex-NBA 7-footer, Marvin Webster aka "The Human Eraser?"

garter snake garters OR the "uniboot"?

YOU MUST CHOOSE!

C H A P T E R 4

COOL AND UNUSUAL PUNISHMENT (DEATHS AND TORTURES)

Uh oh. The Deity's been channel surfing, and, once again, he's not so impressed with the human race. He's about to hit the do-over button. But wait! There is another possibility. A martyr. Someone who can suffer for the pop cultural sins of mankind. Someone like you. And so it will be written that you will suffer a horrendous torture by way of the very same pop culture that has perverted the world and your mind. Fortunately for you, there is a vestige of mercy in the Deity's mind, and he allows you to choose between the lesser of his two evils...

Would you rather...

be machine-gunned to death with Lite-Brite pegs

OR

be wrapped up and suffocated in a giant Fruit Roll-Up?

Would you rather...

pass a kidney stone the size and shape of a GoBot

OR

a Koosh ball?

YOU MUST CHOOSE!

Would you rather spend an eighteen hour car ride with...

K-fed *OR* Britney Spears?

fitness celebrity John Basedow *OR* Omarosa from *The Apprentice*?

Bruce Banner *OR* Star Jones?

Jerry Falwell *OR* Dumb Donald?

Courtney Love *OR* Barbra Streisand?

Ludwig Von Beethoven *OR* Baron Von Raschke?

YOU MUST CHOOSE!

Would you rather fight to the death...

50 Cabbage Patch Dolls *OR* 100 GI Joe action figures?

50 Fry Guys *OR* 50 remote control cars?

the Cocoa Puffs Bird *OR* the Noid?

500 fabric softener sheets *OR* 500 dreidels?

100 cups of coffee *OR* 30 watermelons?

YOU MUST CHOOSE!

Would you rather...

have a Sudoku grid tattoo with attached tattoo needle that was open to the public to try to solve

OR

be covered by a dozen nicotine patch Colorforms that people can put all over your body as they see fit?

YOU MUST CHOOSE!

Would you rather...

be beaten to death with Tinker Toys

OR

killed in avalanche of D&D dice?

Things to consider: the hard edges of a 20-sided crystal, hit points

Would you rather...

enter a cave and be attacked by thousands of Wacky WallWalkers

OR

be eaten alive by the cast of *What's Happenin'*?

Things to consider: adhesiveness of WallWalkers, adhesiveness of Shirley Hemphill, Dr. Fad's lair

YOU MUST CHOOSE!

Would you rather...

receive acupuncture with a nail gun

OR

be placed on a pizza tray and cooked for ten minutes in a Pizza Hut oven?

Things to consider: Why don't books get paid for product placement?

Would you rather...

sleep next to a humidifier full of diarrhea

OR

drink the entire contents of a boxer's post-fight spit bucket?

YOU MUST CHOOSE!

61

Would you rather be stuck on a crowded bus with...

Real World reality "stars" *OR* decaying corpses?

The Brat Pack *OR* the characters from *Fraggle Rock*?

braggadocious upholsterers *OR* jaded warlocks?

bawdy accordion players *OR* alluring zoologists?

wistful Foot Locker employees *OR* pussy-whipped Green Berets?

Would you rather have an airplane seat directly next to...

Fat Albert *OR* B.A. Baracus?

The Invisible Man *OR* Teen Wolf?

Deion Sanders *OR* a woefully insecure Sleestak?

YOU MUST CHOOSE!

Would you rather...

have all of your hook-ups displayed prominently in YouTube videos

OR

all your masturbatory fantasies printed as a Sunday comic in explicit detail?

Would you rather...

be run over by Thomas the Tank Engine

OR

be trampled to death by thousands of My Little Ponies?

YOU MUST CHOOSE!

Would you rather...

be churned to death by a hard-hearted Amish giant

OR

be bombarded by a fatal never-ending barrage of ping pong overhead slams?

Would you rather...

have your lips knitted shut

OR

crocheted shut?

Things to consider: Is there a difference? No really, we'd like to know, is there?
Please email answers to: shutlips@wouldyourather.com

YOU MUST CHOOSE!

Would you rather...

die in a hail storm of croutons

OR

drown in a giant bowl of Campbell's New England clam chowder?

Would you rather...

forcibly floss your teeth with rusty barbed wire

OR

bob for apples in a Long John Silver deep fryer?

YOU MUST CHOOSE!

Would you rather...

saw through your thumbs with a hack saw

OR

slice off your nipples with a deli meat-slicer?

(Borg only) Would you rather...

be assimilated

OR

be assimilated?

Things to consider: Resistance is futile

YOU MUST CHOOSE!

Would you rather...

shave your left eyeball with a Gillette Sensor

OR

pour a gallon of boiling water down your throat?

Would you rather...

be pureed in a giant blender

OR

be tanned to death in an over-charged tanning bed?

YOU MUST CHOOSE!

Would you rather fight to the death...

a creature that has the body of a wolverine and the head of a cobra

OR

a creature that has the body of a tiger and the head of Ed Begley, Jr.?

Would you rather...

fight a creature that had the body of a bull and the head of a lion

OR

a creature that had the body of an eagle, the head of a snake, and the hair of Donald Trump?

YOU MUST CHOOSE!

Would you rather...

be compressed until lifeless in a vice of Bristle Blocks?

OR

be corkscrewed to death?

Would you rather...

be a rodeo clown with a bad leg

OR

Danny Bonaduce's personal assistant?

YOU MUST CHOOSE!

Would you rather...

have Roger Federer forehand your face at full force

OR

have Tiger Woods take a tee-shot to your teeth?

Things to consider: Say that three times fast.

Would you rather...

nap on a waffle iron pillow

OR

have your tonsils Dust-bustered out?

YOU MUST CHOOSE!

71

Would you rather...

be speared with giant Capri Sun straws and then sucked dry

OR

be dragged by your ankles from Mark Martin's car around the Daytona 500 race track?

Would you rather...

be shrunken down and live in a land of a Thomas's English Muffin

OR

in a bowl of Alpha-Bits?

Things to consider: nooks, crannies, and the third lesser-known and most dangerous crevice type: plelsbons!

YOU MUST CHOOSE!

C H A PT E R

MUSIC OF THE SPHERES

"Anything that is too stupid to be spoken is sung." – Voltaire (google it)

The Deity has some questions about Earthly music. Why for example is DJing (in the sense of selecting songs) considered an art form but running a projector is not? Why do you only need a melody for a "hook" now, whereas before a "tune" was kind of a central requirement for a song. Notwithstanding, the Deity has eclectic tastes when it comes to music, as evidenced by a motley assortment of musical dilemmas.

Would you rather...

as a child, be reared by Britney Spears

OR

K-Fed?

Things to consider: driving, "PopoZao" lullabies

Would you rather...

have your life scored by John Williams

OR

have the song "Whoomp There It Is" play at 120 decibels whenever you complete a bowel movement?

Things to consider: using public restrooms

YOU MUST CHOOSE!

Would you rather...

always wear your hair in the style of an 80's big hair band

OR

your pants?

Would you rather...

be limited to N.W.A. tunes when playing goodnight lullabies to your children

OR

be limited to listening to *Barney* songs in the car?

YOU MUST CHOOSE!

Would you rather...

only be able to speak using words contained in contained in Air Supply songs *OR* Black Sabbath songs?

words from the *Gilligan's Island* theme song *OR* the *Cheers* theme song?

words in the song "Macarena" *OR* "Rico Suave"?

Would you rather...

live in a musical in the tone of *High School Musical*

OR

Phantom of the Opera?

YOU MUST CHOOSE!

CHAPTER 6

POWERS AND FANTASIES

The Deity is feeling good. He took mortal form and had relations with several Victoria Secrets models, the Pussycat Dolls, and an aardwolf. And now the Deity, in all his largesse, wants to give back by allowing you the chance to fulfill a fantasy of your own (maybe not your first choice, but a fantasy nonetheless). Better yet, he may bestow upon you a super power. Okay, maybe "super" is a strong word.

Would you rather...

be able to fight and kill masterfully with keys *OR* those paddle and ball toys?

your own spit *OR* your own mustache?

your own pony tail *OR* your computer mouse?

Would you rather...

have the National Anthem changed to Creedence Clearwater Revival's "Down on the Corner"

OR

have the Pledge of Allegiance changed to the lyrics of "I Like Big Butts" by Sir Mix-A-lot?

Things to consider: reciting the Pledge in school, inaugural ceremonies, anthems before sports games, rumors that Sir Mix-A-Lot actually mixes in moderation

YOU MUST CHOOSE!

78

Would you rather...

be able to give someone else the extra weight you should put on after you eat poorly

OR

be able to give your hangovers to someone else after you drink?

YOU MUST CHOOSE!

Would you rather...

hold hands with Rod Carew

OR

catch lightning bugs with Donny Wahlberg?

Would you rather have your eulogy delivered by...

Barak Obama

OR

Foghorn Leghorn?

YOU MUST CHOOSE!

Would you rather...

produce helium-filled feces **OR** TNT-filled feces?

capsul-shelled feces **OR** perfectly cubed feces?

feces that fade away in two minutes **OR** feces that have the personality of Howie Long?

"mood" feces that change color depending on your emotional state **OR** fortune feces (feces that have a secret fortune written in the middle of each piece)?

YOU MUST CHOOSE!

Would you rather...

HAVE YOUR DREAMS WRITTEN AND DIRECTED BY THE MAKERS OF THE MATRIX

OR

BY THE MAKERS OF GIRLS GONE WILD?

83

Would you rather...

be able to summon background singers at any moment

OR

have eyes that can tint themselves like light-sensitive sunglasses?

Would you rather...

have raspberry scented B.O.

OR

hands that can exude lubricant upon command?

YOU MUST CHOOSE!

Would you rather...

have the power to project a Jell-O force field

OR

be able to perfectly gauge cream and sugar amounts by eyeing the color of your coffee?

Would you rather...

have a Tic Tac dispensing nose

OR

be capable of going 0 to 60 in 2.3 seconds?

Things to consider: stopping

YOU MUST CHOOSE!

Would you rather...

be able to record your sex dreams while you sleep for viewing while you're awake

OR

be able to save all of your memories for safe-keeping and easy recall on a USB flash drive?

Would you rather...

have 15 minutes of conversation with Gandhi

OR

15 minutes of unbridled passion with Jessica Alba? Vice versa?

YOU MUST CHOOSE!

Would you rather...

speak in surround sound

OR

have the ability to transform your sexual partner's face into that of the celebrity of your choice for one minute per day?

Would you rather...

be able to fart out Polaroid photos

OR

have self-tying sneakers?

YOU MUST CHOOSE!

87

Would you rather...

be a Transformer who can transform into a George Foreman grill OR a yarmulke?

a Trapper Keeper notebook OR that foot measuring device?

a cement parking space block OR Geraldine Ferraro?

Would you rather...

be able to blow tranquilizer dart snot-rockets

OR

have supersonic hearing but only when people are talking about mulch-related topics?

Things to consider: angle of dart shot, sneezing, mulch fetishists

Would you rather spend a day with...

Paul Revere and Donny Osmond

OR

F. Scott Fitzgerald and Mr. T?

Would you rather...

execute a perfect two-handed Tomahawk dunk over Robert Duvall

OR

dominate Felicity Huffman in Scrabble?

POWERS AND FANTASIES

YOU MUST CHOOSE!

Would you rather...
get drunk-dialed by Abe Lincoln
OR
Johnny Appleseed?

Would you rather...
start a trapeze act with Dianne Feinstein
OR
pickpocket Harmon Killebrew?

YOU MUST CHOOSE!

Would you rather...

have the power of telekinesis but only to alter pants

OR

be able to read minds, but only with people named Deandre?

Would you rather...

have a detachable Fu Manchu mustache/boomerang

OR

"thrusters" on the bottoms of your feet?

Things to consider: rugburn

YOU MUST CHOOSE!

POP Goes the Culture

Super Villains

The Deity likes comic books. And seeing how the producers of *Spiderman*, *X-Men* and the like are pumping out sequel after sequel, and how Hollywood seems dead-set on finding new comic book heroes and villains all the time, the Deity is going to turn you into a super villain, so that you might inspire a movie that he can cash in on.

As a super villain, would you rather be...

The Registrar **OR** The Humidifier?

The Fifth Year Senior **OR** The Male Cheerleader?

The Unitarian **OR** The Ubiquitous Shirtless Guy You Always See On *Cops*?

Captain Condiment **OR** The Guy Who Just Got A Haircut?

The Heckler **OR** The Doorman?

Things to consider: Imagine the uniform, powers, alter egos, and catchphrases for your character

Would You Rather Live in a World Where...

"The world don't move to the beat of just one drum. What might be right for you, might not be right for some." – Ralph Waldo Emerson

Would you rather live in a world...
where all conversation was sung like in a Broadway musical
OR
where all news was delivered by news anchors under 6 years old?

YOU MUST CHOOSE!

Would you rather live in a world where...

golf courses and cemeteries were combined on one property

OR

churches and paintball parks were?

Would you rather live in a world where...

the moon gave out light like a disco ball

OR

where the sun was the big smiling face of Tom Bosley (Mr. Cunningham from *Happy Days*)?

YOU MUST CHOOSE!

Would you rather live in a world without...

TV *OR* your cousins?

Instant Messaging *OR* organized religion?

MTV *OR* PBS?

punctuation *OR* glass?

hip-hop *OR* magic?

Kant's Transcendental Idealism *OR* Jungian archetypal constructs?

YOU MUST CHOOSE!

Would you rather...

grow up in the wild
OR
in a Sbarro's?

Would you rather live in a world...

where wars are settled with soldiers facing off in massive games of Rock, Paper, Scissors
OR
where you can get out of paying parking tickets by beating the judge in one-on-one basketball?

Things to consider: Judge Shawn Bradley

YOU MUST CHOOSE!

Would you rather live in the world of...

The Flintstones **OR** *The Jetsons*?

Narnia **OR** Middle Earth?

a ZZ top video **OR** a Ford truck commercial?

The Iliad **OR** *Sesame Street*?

Sex in the City **OR** *Sin City*?

King of the Hill **OR** *Benny Hill*?

YOU MUST CHOOSE!

Would you rather...

LIVE IN A WORLD WHERE IT RAINED SUPERBALLS

OR

WHERE PEOPLE HAD MR. POTATO HEAD-STYLE FACIAL FEATURES THAT COULD BE REMOVED AND EXCHANGED?

Would you rather...

your life be one big '80's movie shopping montage

OR

one big '80's movie training montage?

Things to consider: your best friend giving your disapproving looks while you try on outfits, vast and triumphant improvement, carrying lots of shopping bags (for both)

YOU MUST CHOOSE!

Would you rather...

live in a house designed by M.C. Escher

OR

MC Hammer?

YOU MUST CHOOSE!

Would you rather live in a world where...

all presidential debates were conducted via battle rap

OR

via ultimate fighting?

Would you rather...

live in the world of *Apocalypto*

OR

be unable to leave the set of the *Ellen Degeneris* show?

YOU MUST CHOOSE!

Would you rather read...

Girls Gone Wild: The Novel

She pried off the water-saturated mini-T-shirt, the last obstinate cling releasing like the inhibition she was shedding.

"Whoooo-hooooo-yeahhhh" bellowed the crowd who below her awaited their daily feeding of lascivious images like seals at Sea World.

"Whooo-hoo, yeahhhhh!" confirmed a posse of drunken members of the Kappa Sig fraternity who teetered on a balcony across the parade-laden street.

Spurred by the wanton courage of her compatriot, the young lady's peer delicately lifted her shirt, exposing part of one breast, and then quickly let the shirt recede to gravity's will.

"Senior's '05!" proffered a young man with vomit crusted on the corner of his mouth.

"Whoooo-Yeahhhhhhhh!" his friend added.

OR

(see next page)

Donkey Kong: The Novel

He leaped with all his might over the rolling barrel, fighting to keep his eyes forward and not lift his gaze toward the captive damsel. The hammer hovering mere inches away, it was time to turn the tables. With a last vestige of energy, Mario grasped for the hammer and seized it with the determination of a plumber who had a problem to fix.

"Oh, if my brother Luigi, could see me now," thought the mustachioed stereotype. BAM! The barrel was no match for the mighty swing of the stout and proud Italian. BAM! Another barrel was lost to the ether. Onward, Mario trod, the slight incline of the steel girder feeling like the slope of the mighty Everest.

And then he heard it. Whether it was the roar of a rolling barrel or the growl of the giant ape, Mario did not know. What he had no doubts about whatsoever was that the sound shook him to his very core.

YOU MUST CHOOSE!

CHAPTER 7

TECHNOLOGY

The Deity is impressed with one particular category of human achievement: technology. Upon further probing, however, the Deity realizes what is responsible for such a rapid rate of technological advancement: porn. Man's insatiable need to access a greater variety and quantity of pornography has resulted in broadband Internet, streaming video, high def DVD, and numerous medical discoveries to augment the body. There must be another way toward innovation. It's time for some divine intervention.

Would you rather...

only be able to write by tattooing on yourself or someone else

OR

only be able to take pictures of your kids and loved ones by scanning them directly into the computer?

Would you rather have on your instant message buddy list...

David Sedaris *OR* Donald Rumsfeld?

Kim Jong-il *OR* porn star Kobe Tai?

Jesus *OR* Steve Kerr?

Things to Consider: WWJIM

YOU MUST CHOOSE!

Would you rather...

have a Blackberry whose smart-type feature always makes racist and bigoted assumptions of what you are typing

OR

have a stuttering automated voice on your cell phone?

Would you rather...

have a retractable stylus for a fingernail

OR

a computer mouse touch pad on your left nipple?

YOU MUST CHOOSE!

Would you rather live in the video game...

Myst *OR* Grand Theft Auto?

Warcraft *OR* Madden NFL Football?

Halo *OR* Zelda?

Final Fantasy *OR* Elevator Action?

Robotron *OR* Kaboom?

Things to consider: frenzy of movement, monotony of moving stacked water buckets back and forth

YOU MUST CHOOSE!

If you could link your brain directly to a website to mentally access all information, video and images at all times, **would you rather be linked to...**

dictionary.com *OR* juggs.com?

mapquest.com *OR* cnn.com?

theonion.com *OR* popsugar.com?

Bunk1.com *OR* Wilwheaton.net?

YOU MUST CHOOSE!

Would you rather...

the only technology you can use be what you had in 1982

OR

the only clothes you can wear be what you had in 1982?

Would you rather...

have your car have a horn like that of the General Lee in *Dukes of Hazzard*?

OR

have a car with a GPS that has the voice of Harry Karry?

YOU MUST CHOOSE!

Would you rather have your cell phone ring function set on...

Sulfur Emission *OR* First Degree Burn?

Marv Albert Yelling "Yes!" *OR* Incredibly Realistic Sounding Gunshot?

Vacuum *OR* Throb?

Self-righteous Bono Speech *OR* Maudlin Nostalgia About Simpler Times On The Fjords?

Itch *OR* Lemon? (note: phone must be in mouth for Lemon to work)

YOU MUST CHOOSE!

Would you rather...

see the world in Xbox graphic quality

OR

hear all conversation as if on a spotty cell phone call?

YOU MUST CHOOSE!

Downward Viral

The Deity loves to surf the net looking for viral videos, especially scandalous celebrity clips. He's file-sharing, but you can only choose one to watch.

Which video would you rather download...

Alan_Thicke's_Cleveland_Steamer.mpg *OR* Ben_Kingsley_Farts_In_Church.avi?

Kofi_Annan_Reads_Aloud_From_Penthouse_Forum.wav *OR*
John_Madden_Vomits_On_Little_Girl.avi?

Peasant_Woman_Has_Sex_With_Abacus_And_Successfully_Computes_Calculation.avi *OR* Dick_Cheney_caught_lipsynching/dancing_to_Oops,_I_Did_It_Again.wmv?

Spelunker_Grinds_Against_Stalagmite.avi *OR*
Spelunker_Grinds_Against_Stalactite.avi?

YOU MUST CHOOSE!

Would you rather...

have an alarm clock that wakes you up by shaking your bed violently *OR* by slowly making the bed ice-cold?

by loudly reminding you of all the problems in your life *OR* by slowly dripping Yoo-Hoo onto your forehead?

by a soothing voice whispering optimistic affirmations *OR* by manually stimulating you with a "Happy Beginning?"

by transporting you to a random place on the planet *OR* by materializing a Mugatu Beast next to you in bed?

YOU MUST CHOOSE!

POP Goes the Culture

HEROES

The Deity likes that show *Heroes*. Like him, the show is well-presented and nerdy, and one of the WYR authors briefly did improv with the Asian guy on it. But to keep it fresh, the Deity feels the show could use a new hero: you.

Would you rather...

have the ability to empty your bladder by "beaming" your urine to a toilet like in *Star Trek*

OR

be capable of shooting pubic "quills" in self-defense like a porcupine?

Would you rather...

be Dr. Grass, a superhero whose power is to induce grass stains

OR

The Summarizer, a superhero who can clearly and concisely express any given situation?

115

CHAPTER 8

MORE SEX

They say that a deity thinks about sex every seven seconds. Consequently, it appears the Deity is not done meddling in the affairs of your love life. He needs to purge the perverse thoughts plaguing his infinite mind, and you again are his guinea pig.

Would you rather have sex with...

just the top half of Jessica Alba

OR

just the bottom half of Jessica Alba?

Would you rather...

administer oral sex to the Phillie Phanatic

OR

dry hump Count Chocula?

YOU MUST CHOOSE!

Would you rather...

have Nicholas Sparks write you a love letter

OR

be serenaded by Biz Markie?

Things to consider: Does Nicholas Sparks got what you need? How many of you started singing "You say he's just a friend, yeah you say he's just a friend... Oh baby youuuuu..." Now you have that song stuck in your head.

"The club was jumpin and word is bond
I saw girls walkin around with jeans painted on
Splittin they skirts up the middle, tight leather and lace
Both me and Jimmy agree, we're gonna like this place"

— Walter Mondale, upon first entering the White House

YOU MUST CHOOSE!

Would you rather use as sex toys...

a wooden duck, a trident, and some balsamic vinaigrette

OR

a piano tie, a bag of croutons, a Gumby doll, and a Ronald Reagan mask?

Would you rather...

have an internal voice-over and montage where that *Inside the NFL* guy recounts and summarizes your sex life at the end of each week

OR

have a voice-over and montage where the melodramatic Dr. Meredith Grey from *Grey's Anatomy* thematically ties up your emotional and philosophical experiences each week?

YOU MUST CHOOSE!

Would you rather have sex with...

Tom Brady

OR

Webster if they exchanged heights?

Would you rather have sex with...

Pierce Brosnan

OR

Flavor Flav if they switched voices and demeanors?

YOU MUST CHOOSE!

121

Would you rather...

your G-spot be located in your esophagus

OR

on each of your finger tips? Your eyeball? Ralph Macchio's forearm?

Things to consider: typing, swallowing, looming image of avuncular Pat Morita

Would you rather...

have a lover who is 6'4" with 32A breasts

OR

4'5" with 42HHH breasts? 3'2" with 66N breasts? 2'1" with 98ZZZZ breasts?

YOU MUST CHOOSE!

Would you rather...

have nipples that constantly twirl like pinwheels

OR

testicles that swing back and forth like a pendulum?

Would you rather...

have sex with Tim Russert

OR

a 50% scale Brad Pitt?

Things to consider: Pitt's shrunken genitals, rumors Russert is hung like a horse

YOU MUST CHOOSE!

123

Would you rather have sex with...

Johnny Depp himself **OR** Johnny Depp as Captain Jack Sparrow from *Pirates of the Carribean*?

Jim Carrey himself **OR** Jim Carrey as *The Mask*?

Leonard Nimoy himself **OR** Leonard Nimoy as Spock from *Star Trek*?

Would you rather have sex with...

Halle Berry herself **OR** Halle Berry as Storm from *X-Men*?

Sharon Stone herself **OR** Sharon Stone as her character in *Basic Instinct*?

Elizabeth Berkeley in *Showgirls* **OR** Elizabeth Berkeley in *Saved by the Bell*?

Things to consider: are you going to hell?

YOU MUST CHOOSE!

Would you rather...

have your love emails posted on Google's home page

OR

have the soundtrack to your love-making be available as an iTunes Podcast for download?

Would you rather...

have sex with an Indian Gwyneth Paltrow

OR

a severely parched Avril Lavigne?

MORE SEX

YOU MUST CHOOSE!

125

Would you rather your only porn be...

John Hughes films *OR* Pert-Plus commercials?

sex symbols of the 70's *OR* 50's and 60's?

video game vixens *OR* imprecise memories of Deborah Norville circa 1985?

fraternity guys bragging to each other about the chicks they nailed *OR*
a Big & Tall catalog?

Three's Company double entendre *OR* medical diagnoses on *House*?

MythBusters' experiments *OR* Lakers box scores?

YOU MUST CHOOSE!

Would you rather have sex with...

Penn *OR* Teller?

Ashley *OR* Mary-Kate Olsen?

Deepak Chopra *OR* Tupac Shakur?

an oiled-up Deborah Messing *OR* a glow-in-the dark Jodie Foster?

Ex-Dallas Maverick, Rolando Blackman *OR* current New York Knick Rolando Balkman?

Tobey Maguire *OR* Jake Gyllenhaal? Is there a difference?

Would you rather...

have sex with Daphne from *Scooby Doo*

OR

kill Scrappy Doo?

YOU MUST CHOOSE!

Date, Marry, Screw?

Borat, Ali G, Bruno

Pauly Shore, John Kerry, Jeffrey Dahmer

Nicole Richie, Tara Reid, Paris Hilton

Randy Jackson, Paula Abdul, Simon Cowell

Drunk Lindsay Lohan, sober Lindsay Lohan, strung-out Lindsay Lohan

Date, Marry, Screw, Head-butt, Re-enact a Civil War Battle Against, or Eat Pork With?

Matthew Perry, Emeril Lagasse, Steve Buscemi, Latrell Sprewell, Stephen Hawking, Justin Timberlake?

Sarah Silverman, Sharon Osborne, Sally Jesse Raphael, Joan of Arc, Ann Coulter, Mia Hamm?

David Copperfield, Mark Wahlberg, Tony Little, Steven Segal, Gomberg, Sesame Street's Count von Count?

YOU MUST CHOOSE!

Back to Reality

Everybody has a reality show idea. Even the Deity pitched a show about a group of quarreling gods in the pantheon. He said it was "Real World Meets the Bible." But network execs said it wouldn't play in the heartland. Undaunted, the Deity has some new ideas...

Would you rather watch...

America's Most Pensive Ruminations **OR** *Alzheimer's Patients Say the Darndest Things!*?

Survivor: Home Depot **OR** *Europe's Funniest Defenestrations*?

Close Quarters – "Members of rival gangs are handcuffed to Gary Player" **OR** *The Mormon Bachelor* – "50 women compete to win the heart of the Bachelor, but only 3-5 can win?"

MORE SEX

Would you rather...

have sex with a woman with Dr. Ruth Westheimer's body on the top half and Heidi Klum's body on the bottom half

OR

Heidi Klum's on top and Grimace's body on the bottom?

Would you rather...

have breast implants made of Jell-O

OR

that stress ball material?

YOU MUST CHOOSE!

CHAPTER 9

DEITY'S GREATEST HITS VOLUME 4: ELECTRIC BOOGALOO 3

The Deity isn't going to wait for *American Idol* to discover and market him in a carefully calculated process of public mind-control. The Deity is an artist. He's releasing another "Best of" compilation on his Indie label, a comprehensive collection of deranged dilemmas of all sorts to make you think and squirm.

Would you rather...

sneeze with the force of a double barrel shotgun

OR

fart with the same force?

Things to consider: whiplash, "shrapnel"

Would you rather...

have Twizzlers for hair

OR

Sharpee permanent markers for fingers?

Things to consider: irresistible tendency to smell your fingers, ravenous co-workers, scratching your back

YOU MUST CHOOSE!

Would you rather...

have sex with R2D2

OR

C3PO?

Things to consider: hologram projections, dirty talk in over six millions forms of communication

Would you rather...

be cooked and hardened into a Shrinky Dink

OR

have your body surgically opened and filled with hundreds of wasps?

YOU MUST CHOOSE!

Would you rather fight to the death...

The Rock *OR* fifteen clones of Barbara Bush?

Jackie Chan *OR* the entire Mormon Tabernacle Choir?

3 Broke Ass Stuarts *OR* 10 Mona Lisas come-to-life?

Ryan Seacrest *OR* 22 Q-Berts?

Would you rather...

be a were-parrot (every full moon morph into a parrot)

OR

be a were-gumbel (every full moon morph into Greg Gumbel)?

YOU MUST CHOOSE!

Would you rather...

have a permanent "Got Milk" moustache

OR

have small holes in your cheeks that allowed fluids to leak through like a strainer?

Would you rather...

only be able to exit buildings through the window

OR

be limited in wardrobe to conquistador garb?

YOU MUST CHOOSE!

Would you rather...

only be able to pleasure yourself with your feet

OR

have to select all your meals off of the "Kid's Menu"?

Would you rather...

have an overdramatic reality show based on your neighborhood

OR

your workplace?

YOU MUST CHOOSE!

Would you rather...

cc: Peter O'Toole on all your emails

OR

begin every sentence with "Lord knows...?"

Would you rather...

anything you write vanish after 20 seconds

OR

have any words you say after the first three words in a sentence come out in Aramaic?

YOU MUST CHOOSE!

Would you rather...

wake up each day alternating between before and after weight-loss photos

OR

have foam "You're #1" hands in place of your hands?

Things to consider: maintaining a relationship, having two sets of clothes

Would you rather...

feel nothing but indignation towards people named Franz

OR

constantly feel as though you are being sucked in by a strong undertow?

YOU MUST CHOOSE!

Yes, we understand you can do *Would you rather..?* questions with really gross things...

Would you rather...

suck on a pubic hair gobstopper

OR

eat Cracker Jacks full of scabs?

Would you rather...

consume a Big Mac, vomit it up, re-cook it and eat it again as sauce for a bowl of spaghetti

OR

replace the vanilla fillings in a box of Oreo cookies with a layer of fat from your thigh and then eat them?

YOU MUST CHOOSE!

Would you rather...

have regular sex with Eva Longoria

OR

have regular sex with Rachel Ray and have her cook for you each night?

YOU MUST CHOOSE!

Would you rather...

have sopping wet palms

OR

have your own face when facing forward but have Ted Koppel's profile?

Things to consider: constant pestering from strangers on the street, computer typing, petting zoos

Would you rather...

be haunted by the ghost of Vince Lombardi

OR

by the voice of Tom Carvel?

Things to consider: pressure to win, Fudgie the Whale

YOU MUST CHOOSE!

Would you rather...

have a hairline receding from the back of your head

OR

a receding hairline from the left side of your head? How about a hairline that recedes and proceeds throughout the day like the tides?

Would you rather...

be stuck in an elevator with brawny podiatrists *OR* glamorous roofers?

swanky astronauts *OR* combative landscape architects?

dashing actuaries *OR* domineering statisticians?

YOU MUST CHOOSE!

Would you rather be a Siamese twin...

with Steven Colbert *OR* Jerome Bettis?

John McEnroe *OR* Eminem?

Al Gore *OR* Captain Lou Albano?

YOU MUST CHOOSE!

Would you rather...

have *Law & Order* disease where you discover a dead body every morning

OR

A-Team syndrome, where you get out of all your predicaments with resourceful welding sequences?

Which cartoon would you rather see...

George Washington Carver: Superspy

OR

Popeye: Domestic Abuser?

YOU MUST CHOOSE!

Would you rather...

have a three-way with Dustin Hoffman and Dustin Diamond OR Leon Spinks and Ponce De Leon?

Brooke Burke and Delta Burke OR Halle Berry and Franken Berry?

Gilbert Gottfried and Melissa Gilbert OR Brandy Alexandre and Alexander Graham Bell with a watersports cameo by Alexander Hamilton?

Lucy Liu and Lou Ferrigno OR Paula Abdul and ex-pro wrestler, Abdullah the Butcher?

YOU MUST CHOOSE!

In the *Great American Race*, would you rather be partnered with...

Lionel Richie *OR* Nick Nolte?

Lance Armstrong *OR* David Blaine?

Hannity *OR* Colmes?

Green Lantern *OR* SuperMan?

Hank the Angry Drunken Dwarf *OR* ABBA?

On *The Apprentice*, would you rather have on your team...

Rush Limbaugh *OR* Rob Reiner?

The Zodiac Killer *OR* Iranian President Mahmoud Ahmadinejad?

Warren Buffet *OR* Steve Jobs?

Abagail Adams *OR* Harriet Tubman?

YOU MUST CHOOSE!

Would you rather...

automatically emit a telephone busy signal when someone you're not interested in tries to pick you up

OR

hiccup the Punch-Out arcade game's "Body blow!"?

YOU MUST CHOOSE!

Would you rather...

only be able to communicate with family members by leaving notes on Internet porn message boards

OR

have an ice cream cone wafer face?

(*Star Wars* nerds only) Would you rather...

be carbon frozen á la Han Solo

OR

fall into a Sarlacc pit?

YOU MUST CHOOSE!

Would you rather...

have a Fonzerelli-esque like ability to activate and repair juke-boxes and similar electronic products with the rapping of your fist

OR

have the power to receive and "read" emails in your brain (i.e. without having to use a computer)?

Would you rather...

be incredibly good-looking from eight to ten feet away (but not closer or further)

OR

have your morning always be in the pleasant tone of coffee commercial?

YOU MUST CHOOSE!

Would you rather...

instinctively volley anything thrown to you

OR

foam up with suds and lather like a bubble bath when wet?

Would you rather...

have cellulite of the face

OR

have moss-covered limbs?

YOU MUST CHOOSE!

Would you rather...

experience a phenomenon when you turn off the lights, the theme to *Shaft* plays for 15 seconds

OR

a delusional mentality that causes you to air guitar indefinitely in the presence of the elderly?

Would you rather have your funeral...

written and produced by people who make Spanish variety shows

OR

by John Woo?

YOU MUST CHOOSE!

Would you rather...

excrete celebrity-resembling bowel movements

OR

be able to determine a person's religion be slapping them?

Would you rather...

have Rollerblade feet

OR

telescoping eyes?

YOU MUST CHOOSE!

Would you rather...

as you consume alcohol, gradually begin to think you are Chuck Woolery

OR

as you the day goes on, become convinced you are Gimli from *Lord of the Rings*?

Things to consider: the golden treetops of Lothlorien, being back in "two and two"

YOU MUST CHOOSE!

153

Would you rather...

have to do a single jumping jack at least once every 90 seconds or explode

OR

have to quote Alexander Pushkin once every 30 minutes or be instantly teleported back in time 3 million years (quotes must be different)?

Would you rather...

have sex with Britney Spears with a shaved head **OR** Mischa Barton with a soul patch?

Hilary Swank **OR** a mute Salma Hayek?

Madeline Albright **OR** Bridget Moynahan while she's in labor?

the Dog Whisperer and all the dogs on his show **OR**
Iron Chef Morimoto and the food of the day—"baby octopus"?

Posh Spice and David Beckham **OR** Jay-Z and Beyoncé?

YOU MUST CHOOSE!

Would you rather...

only be allowed to communicate to your children through Power Point presentations

OR

always have to raise your hand and be called on before asking any question?

Would you rather...

have limbs that fluctuated in regards to their length and thickness each day

OR

die if you are not within 200 feet of Mario Van Peebles?

YOU MUST CHOOSE!

Would you rather see as a museum exhibit...

The Air And Space Museum's *Turbulence Simulation Urinals* **OR** The Museum Of Modern Art's "50 Turtles Stuck To The Ceiling With An Unreliable Glue."?

The Mona Lisa Bonet **OR** IMAX film: *Airplane Seat Upholstery: Past To Present*?

Would you rather see as a museum exhibit...

The Pro Bowling Hall Of Fame's "Stick Your Finger In Pro Bowler's Balls" **OR** The National Zoo's "Feel What It's Like To Be Born Out Of An Elephant"?

The Museum Of American History's "Jean Shorts: An Evolution" **OR** the Museum of Natural History Presents George Washington Carver's Peanut Shoes?

YOU MUST CHOOSE!

Would you rather...

have working minute and second hands radiating from your nipples

OR

have Swiffers for feet?

Would you rather...

have a profile where when you turn to the left you appear as Jerry Springer and turn to the right you appear as Harry Hamlin

OR

appear as Carrie Underwood from the front and Michael Clarke Duncan from behind?

YOU MUST CHOOSE!

Would you rather...

have a speech disorder where you say "klelpers" for any word longer than eight letters

OR

any time you enter a room, be painlessly but inevitably and without delay knocked over by a running pig?

YOU MUST CHOOSE!

Would you rather...

all your email exchanges have to be written in toddler talk *OR* jive?

double entendre *OR* with alliteration?

nonlinear differential equation notation *OR* C++?

Would you rather...

have your stomach hair connected to the hair on a stranger's head

OR

have a gum disease that causes you to lose or gain a tooth when the word "Eisenhower" is spoken in your presence?

YOU MUST CHOOSE!

Would you rather...

every few hours, have large, thick afros spontaneously sprout from various parts of your body

OR

be mysteriously compelled to say "ARRR" in a pirate's voice, before every sentence you speak?

Would you rather...

have hair made of ethernet cabling

OR

have tetherballs for breasts?

YOU MUST CHOOSE!

Would you rather...

have a 23" tongue

OR

be utterly convinced that you live within the video game Yar's revenge?

YOU MUST CHOOSE!

Would you rather...

cut off the tips of your fingers with a band saw

OR

consume, in one seating, three-hundred Three Musketeers bars?

Would you rather...

any time someone asks you a question and you don't know the answer, a hundred artichokes fall from above onto you

OR

have a skin bacteria whereby any metal object you touch instantly turns to Sugar Smacks?

YOU MUST CHOOSE!

Would you rather...

have a spouse that only has sex with you while s/he is bitterly ranting about their mother-in-law

OR

while s/he is debating the plausibility of Hausdorf's paradox?

Would you rather...

LeBron James dunk a ball as hard as he can onto your face repeatedly

OR

take a slapshot in the sternum from any of the multitude of anonymous white pro hockey players with a mullet and a weird accent?

YOU MUST CHOOSE!

Yes, we understand you can do serious WYR questions too:

Would you rather...

earn $50,000 a year while all your peers earned $25,000

OR

earn $100,000 while all your peers earned $250,000?

Would you rather...

be immortal but never fall in love

OR

live to 75 with a fulfilling marriage and family?

Would you rather...

have a competent grasp of fiddling, but harbor a closeted affinity for sitting on muffins

OR

build muscle with relative ease, but have the inside of your knee be possessed by Big John Studd?

YOU MUST CHOOSE!

164

Would you rather...

become incredibly boring on Thursdays

OR

upon finishing using a public restroom, feel compelled to utter in a childish voice, "My poopies"?

Would you rather...

have a 3-D topographical map skin

OR

pupils that are Doppler weather maps of the Gulf Coast?

YOU MUST CHOOSE!

About The Authors

Justin Heimberg is a comedy writer who has written for all media including movies, TV, books, and magazines. He, along with David Gomberg, runs Falls Media, an entertainment company specializing in providing short and funny creative services and products.

David Gomberg is notably different from other oozes. Being a growth, he is fixed to one place and cannot move or attack. For the most part, he is forced to feed off of vegetable, organic or metallic substances in an underground wall. If he grows on a ceiling, however, he can sense if someone passes below, and drops onto them. Living creatures touched by Gomberg eventually turn into Gomberg themselves. Gomberg is vulnerable to light, heat, frost, and cure disease spells. Gomberg is mindless and cannot speak. As such, he is regarded as neutral in alignment. Gomberg will re-grow if even the tiniest residue remains, and can germinate to form a full sized ooze again years later.

The Authors, Ten Years Later

Heimberg has gone from posing with artificially forlorn expressions to posing with artificially pensive expressions.

Gomberg's smile is no more, and he now has a balance disorder that causes him to lean slightly forward.

About the Deity

The ringmaster/MC/overlord of the *Would You Rather...* empire is "the Deity." Psychologically and physically a cross between Charles Manson and Gabe Kaplan, the Deity is the one responsible for creating and presenting the WYR dilemmas. It is the Deity who asks **"Would you rather... watch a porno movie with your parents or a porno movie starring your parents?"** And it is the Deity who orders, without exception, that you must choose. No one knows exactly why he does this; suffice to say, it's for reasons beyond your understanding. The Deity communicates with you not through speech, nor telepathy, but rather through several sharp blows to the stomach that vary in power and location. Nearly omnipotent, often ruthless, and obsessed with former NBA seven-footers, the Deity is a random idea generator with a peculiar predilection for intervening in your life in the strangest ways.

Other *Would You Rather...?*® Books:

Would You Rather...?: Love & Sex asks you to ponder such questions as:

- **Would you rather...** orgasm once every ten years OR once every ten seconds?

- **Would you rather...** have to have sex in the same position every night OR have to have sex in a different position every night (you can never repeat)?

- **Would you rather...** have breast implants made of Nerf® OR Play-Doh®?

- **Would you rather...** have sex with the new Daisy Duke (Jessica Simpson) OR classic Daisy Duke (Catherine Bach)?

- **Would you rather...** vicariously experience all orgasms that occur in your zip code OR during sex, have the Microsoft paper clip help icon appear with sex tips?

Would You Rather...?: Love & Sex can be read alone or played together as a game. Laugh-out-loud funny, uniquely imaginative, and deceptively thought-provoking, *Would You Rather...?: Love & Sex* is simultaneously the authors most mature and immature work yet!

Would You Rather...?® 2: Electric Boogaloo
Another collection of over three hundred absurd alternatives and demented dilemmas. Filled with wacky wit, irreverent humor and twisted pop-culture references.

Available at www.wouldyourather.com

Available Starting Fall 2007

Would You Rather...?: Illustrated — Tired of having to visualize these dilemmas yourself? No need anymore with this book of masterfully illustrated ***Would You Rather...?*** dilemmas. Now you can see what it looks like to be attacked by hundreds of Pilsbury Doughboys, get hole-punched to death, sweat cheese, or have pubic hair that grows an inch every second. A feast for the eyes and imagination, ***Would You Rather...?: Illustrated*** gives Salvador Dali a run for his money.

Would You Rather...?'s What's Your Price?
Would you punch your grandmother in the stomach as hard as you can for $500,000? There are no wrong answers but hundreds of "wrong" question in another irresistibly irreverent book of questions from the authors of the ***Would You Rather...?*** series.

Would You Rather...?'s What Would You Be?
Stretch your metaphor muscles along with your imagination as you answer and discuss thought/humor-provoking questions like: If you were a Smurf, which one would you be? What if you were a type of dog? A road sign? A Beatle? A nonsense sound?

Got Your Own *Would You Rather...?* Question?

Go to **www.wouldyourather.com** to submit your question and share it with others. Read and debate thousands of other dilemmas submitted by the authors and users.

www.wouldyourather.com

Featuring:
New *Would you rather...?* questions

More humor books and games

More *Would You Rather...?* products

Comedy videos, writing, animations and more!